Pub & Shop
Fronts of Ireland

Dedicated to Maureen, John, Debbie, Alan
. . . Irish eyes are always smiling !

This edition published 1995 by
John Hinde Limited,
Dublin 18, Ireland.
under licence from The Ugly Duckling Co. Limited.

Paintings by Róisín O'Shea © Róisín O'Shea 1995
This edition © Róisín O'Shea 1995
Text © The Ugly Duckling Co. Limited.
Edited by Donald Sutherland and Róisín O'Shea.

Acknowledgments:
Caitriona Foley and Marie Mulligan,
research assistants.

An Artists Portfolio

Pub & Shop Fronts of Ireland

A Collection of Pen & Ink & Watercolour
paintings by Irish artist Róisín O'Shea.

Born in Cork, Ireland in 1960, Róisín O'Shea studied at the National College of Art and Design, Dublin, and following graduation headed to Sydney, Australia, where she completed a post-graduate diploma in the City Art Institute. On her return in 1985 she continued painting, drawing her inspiration from her native landscape which continues to captivate her today. In her 19 years of painting Róisín has built up an enormous collection of sketches, paintings and photographs from the length and breadth of Ireland which led to this series of books.

INTRODUCTION

I painted my first pub front at the age of fifteen and for the next few years my work almost exclusively featured pub and shop fronts of Ireland. I sold these paintings to pay my way through art college in Dublin and when I went to Sydney, Australia, to study I found that this same subject matter of Irish buildings was again in demand in local galleries. I have travelled extensively in the world and have yet to find streetscapes that inspire me as much as those of my native land. By the time I was in my mid-twenties, almost two-thirds of the subject matter I had painted had gone. It became a kind of mission to seek out 'old' Ireland and preserve it. Although there is now a much greater realisation of the value of our heritage I still feel the urgency to record as many of these buildings as I can. This book is the first volume of a series which will contain some of the thousands of pub and shop fronts that have caught my eye.

Róisín O'Shea

BOLAND'S, KINSALE, CORK

This fine Italianate Doric building was called Barry's Place, named after the Barry brothers who built it in 1878 as a shop with living accommodation overhead. They were followed in 1938 by the Acton family, who established a newsagency there and lived there until 1976. It was then bought by Tony and Colette Boland who, with their family, developed the existing business and established an Irish Craft Shop. Everything sold in the shop is made in Ireland, including fine art prints of my own work portraying local scenes.

SPANIARD PUB, KINSALE, CORK

The Spaniard was established 345 years ago. One family, the Colemans, owned it for over 200 years. The pub of course got its name from the Spanish invasion of 1601. It is actually built on the ruins of a castle overlooking the town. Of the many colourful characters who frequented the bar, a notorious lady called Minnie the Trick is fondly remembered for her famous 'three card trick'. The pub's atmosphere was enhanced by the fishermen who used to come in to sell their daily catch or try and trade it for a few pints. There is a small three-foot door in the wall behind the bar and legend has it that this is a door for the 'little people' to enter and leave the pub by. Although somebody has yet to see these people, the story still persists and the owner, Pat, is telling no different.

JOE TAYLOR, MOYASTA, CLARE

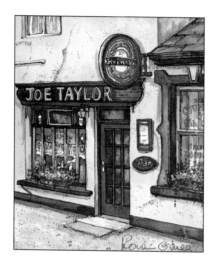

The deeds of this pub go back as far as 1820, but it is thought that the Taylor family (current owners) were here long before that, perhaps as far back as the 1780s. Joe Taylor is now heavily involved in getting the railway back into Moyasta and will happily entertain travellers with the house speciality, a local brew called a mulled pint of Guinness. On a cold day the old railway workers would heat their innards by putting a hot poker from the fire into their pint and adding a teaspoon of ginger. The turf fire is still there – tell Joe I sent you!

FANNY O'DEA'S, LISSYCASEY, CLARE

This is Clare's oldest hostelry, dating back to 1790. Fanny O'Dea came into possession of her drinks licence in an unusual way. One winter's night over two hundred years ago, a High Court Judge, Robert Vere O'Brien, was travelling from Kilrush to Ennis. He stopped off with his coachman at Fanny O'Dea's to shelter from the driving rain. Well-known for her gracious hospitality, she made them very welcome, allowing them to dry their clothes by the roaring turf fire while she prepared some of her famous egg flip laced with whiskey. After several of these warming drinks, the judge, noticing the alcohol content, asked whether or not she had a licence to sell spirits. Fanny told him that she could not afford the licence and that she only gave the drink to her friends. The judge then produced a form, signed it and handed it to Fanny, saying, 'there is your licence, now you may sell intoxicating drink'. The place has had a licence ever since. You can still try the famous egg flip, made to the same 200-year-old secret recipe.

Róisín O'Dea

SEANACHAÍ, DUNGARVAN, WATERFORD

A traditional pub with a reputation for good music and food, it is situated near a 19th century famine gravesite.

THE MARINE BAR, RING, WATERFORD

Famous for its great traditional music sessions, the Marine Bar cannot be missed for its great 'craic' and good company. The bar is owned by Christy, who is also the resident singer/guitarist and master of ceremonies. I have spent many evenings in Ring singing my heart out and have been honoured to join in sessions with Caroline and Mick McKenna who, in particular, cannot be bettered on the squeezebox. Tell Christy that I sent you along and I guarantee you a welcome that would be hard to surpass.

EGG DEPOT, DUBLIN

Based in Wexford Street, Dublin, this shop has tempted me again and again over the years – I cannot resist painting it. The shop itself has stayed the same over time, it is the shops on either side that keep changing. It is certainly one of the smallest shops I have come across.

HYNES PUB, DUBLIN

I was asked by well-known publican Dessie Hynes to paint a picture of my ideal pub. I did and he duly built it, much to my surprise. Hynes pub is at Baggot Street Bridge, and is hard to miss with the enormous cartoon pints of Guinness up above the pub front.

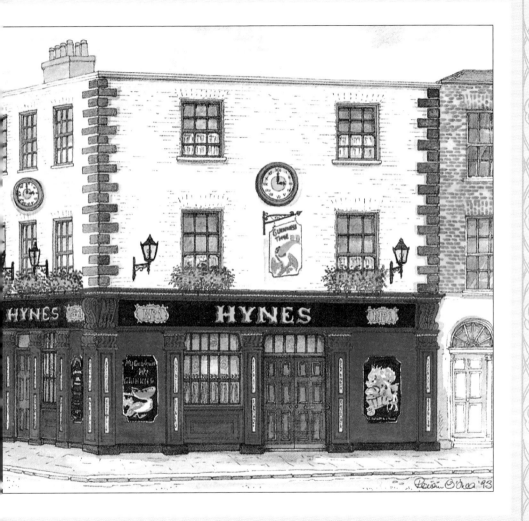

T. GUNNING'S ANTIQUES, LIMERICK CITY

The deeds of this building show that it was built on the site of an old racquet court. A recent discovery during some digging revealed a beautiful cobblestoned area in the garden to the rear of this building. This tennis court was probably built for the military personnel of King John's Castle about 1,000 years ago. Beside the antique shop, the castellated structure is now the old toll house where you had to pay a ha'penny to bring your cow across the bridge.

CURIOS, DUBLIN

This little shop has already disappeared since I did the painting. Located at 30 Wellington Quay, it is being demolished for development of the Temple Bar area.

BEWLEY'S, DUBLIN

Bewley's is a unique meeting place in Dublin. More than just a coffee shop, it is constantly alive and buzzing with excited chatter against a backdrop of old world elegance. During college it was mandatory to spend as much time as possible 'hanging out' and drinking coffee. Literary greats such as James Joyce and Patrick Kavanagh were known to while away the hours in a similar fashion. The Bewleys were of French extraction. After settling in Ireland in 1700 the Bewleys became a very successful business family. In 1835 Charles Bewley arranged for the importation of 2,099 tea chests into Ireland. It proved to be a lucrative move and more transactions such as this followed. Tea became part of the staple diet of Irish people, both rich and poor. The cafés as we know them were created almost by accident. Coffee in 1894 was relatively unknown. Ernest Bewley decided to create some interest in the product by holding a coffee-making demonstration; his wife made scones and buns to serve it with, and the idea of a coffee shop was born. In 1927, Bewley's of Grafton Street was opened.

THE QUEENS, DALKEY

A very popular pub with the under forties, Queens is beside Dalkey Castle on the main street of Dalkey village. The Irish for Dalkey is Delginis, which means Thorn Island. The Danes, who had a fortress here in the 10th century, gave Dalkey its present name, changing Delg to Dalk and Inis to Ey.

DICK MACK'S PUB, DINGLE, KERRY

Oliver is the third generation McDonnell to own this pub/haberdashery shop. It has the distinction of probably being the only pub in Ireland that also offers a shoe repair service, introduced about 1930. I have purchased two pairs of wellington boots and a personalised leather key-ring while enjoying a chat and a pint, over the years.

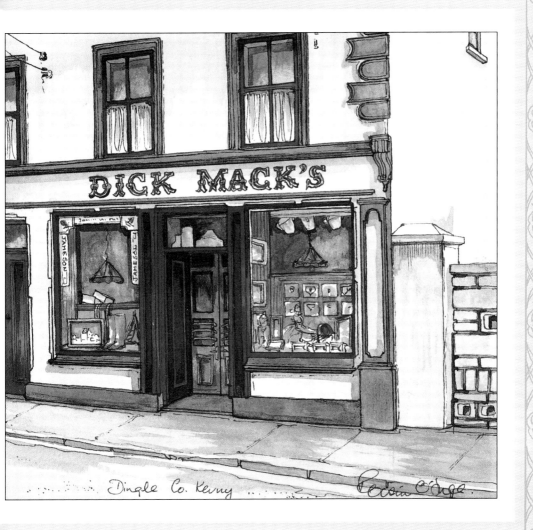

Dingle Co. Kerry

BUTTERFIELD, KILDARE

This pub is in the middle of a small Quaker village called Balitore in County Kildare. The village had a feeling of a place that time had forgotten and the pub's exterior intrigued me; I intend to revisit Balitore and spend some time understanding the village's history.

KITTY O'SHEA'S, DUBLIN

I had my very first solo exhibition as an artist in Kitty O'Shea's pub in 1983 which helped me raise the airfare for Australia where I finished my studies. I still smile when I think of myself and Brian Loughney on our hands and knees painting the floor the night before the exhibition opened. The Loughney brothers, Kevin and Brian, can be proud of a pub that is steeped in traditional values, music, food and 'craic'. The brothers have expanded their Irish empire with pubs in Paris, Brussels and Barcelona.

WHELAN, LAOIS

This type of shop front is fast becoming a rare sight in Ireland, especially in the last ten years. It caught my eye and I painted it.

O'HARE'S ANCHOR BAR AND GROCER, CARLINGFORD, LOUTH

In the O'Hare family since 1860, this pub is one of the very few remaining pub-cum-grocershops, where you can get a pint of Guinness and a bag of sugar under the one roof. P. J. O'Hare was a great storyteller in his day and told a great yarn about the suit of Leprechaun clothes he found one day while walking up the mountains. Whether he simply came across it or wrestled it off the poor Leprechaun I don't know. The suit is still in the bar today, kept safely behind a glass case – I suppose in case the Leprechaun comes back looking for it!

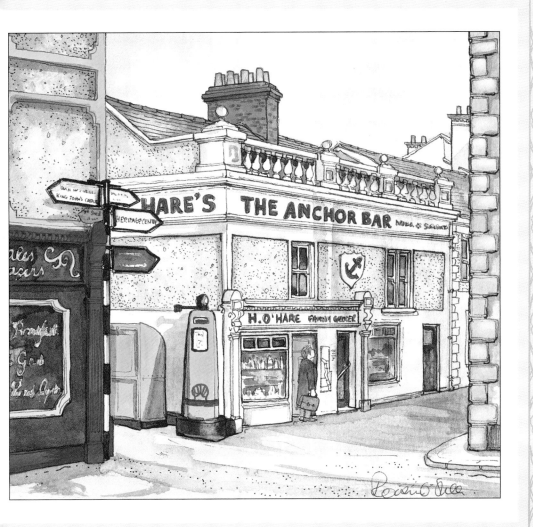

THE CIGAR DIVAN, CARLOW TOWN

This shop has been in Mrs. Hartnett's family since 1822 and was passed along three generations. The shop still retains its old world feel. The shop was opened in a time when the tobacco shop was very much a social centre and customers were welcome to drop in to pass the time of day. Along one of the walls was a long settee or divan (hence the name) on which the men would sit and enjoy a leisurely smoke from a wide range of the finest tobaccos while discussing all the local news.

GODFREY'S, ENNISCORTHY, WEXFORD

The shop was established in 1835. The original owners, the Godfreys, left in 1910 to move permanently to Belfast and the O'Briens then took it over. It was passed down to current owner John Byrne by his mother. The shop front still remains as it was back in the time of the Godfreys.

J. MALONE HAIRDRESSER, CLANE, KILDARE

The village of Clane came 2nd in a group of the Tidy Towns competition. Although this building may not exactly blend in with the neat rows of houses and tidy gardens, it certainly lends a certain amount of charm to the town, and possesses a unique character of its own. It would be a great shame to see it go. However, the owner has applied for planning permission to rebuild on the site, so perhaps this painting will serve as a reminder of this quaint old building.

HIGH CROSS INN, KILDARE

A good rest point on the road to Carlow, this pub has always intrigued me; unfortunately I was unable to get the history of the pub, but it is worth a visit to see its old style interior and have a bite to eat.

SKEFFINGTON ARMS, GALWAY

The Skeffington Arms Hotel is situated on Eyre Square in Galway city which is well-known for its festivals, good music and restaurants. John F. Kennedy was the first American president to visit Ireland while still in office and received the freedom of Galway city a few months before he was assassinated in 1963. The square contains the John F. Kennedy Memorial Park.

TIGH NEACHTAIN, GALWAY CITY

This medieval building was for over 500 years the town house of the Martin family, the biggest landowners in Ireland. They owned about a half a million acres from Clifden to Galway town. Present owner Jimmy Martin is third generation Neachtain to run the pub. His grandfather bought it exactly 100 years ago, in October 1894. It remains in the same traditional state today, the only addition being the acquisition of the building next door into which the pub has been extended to form a large snug. The extension is from the same era as the pub and is very much in keeping with the feel of the whole place. Neachtain's is famous for its traditional music sessions, and when Jimmy was asked whether anybody famous had played there, he said that everybody goes there – but he's not telling, he's going to keep his secrets until he decides to write a book.

Galway

Seán O'Mea

HAIRDRESSERS, SLIGO TOWN

THE THATCH PUB, BALLISODARE, SLIGO

Originally a private home, The Thatch was licenced in 1828 when it was a coaching inn. It has been in the same family for over 300 years – the official deeds go back as far as 1828. As a coaching inn, The Thatch was used as a halfway stop to refresh both people and animals on the journey to Sligo town from places such as Collooney and Dromard, in the days when this fifteen to twenty-mile trip was a strenuous journey.

THE CROWN LIQUOR SALOON, BELFAST

The Crown Liquor Saloon is a famous haunt for the theatre crowd. Actors, actresses and singers can be regularly seen relaxing in the bar after a show in the nearby Grand Opera House. This beautiful pub has a carefully-restored Victorian interior. It is a feast of bright-coloured tiling, mirrors and marble, intimate snugs and elaborate wood panelling. In 1978, the National Trust took the unusual step of acquiring The Crown with a view to restoring it to its traditional style. Interior shots of the bar can be seen in the 1947 film 'Odd Man Out' by Carol Reed, and it was from these shots that the intricate details were copied. Photos of the set, a construction in Pinewood Studios, also helped to piece the whole look together.

BIRDYS NEWSAGENTS, CARRICKMACROSS, MONAGHAN

Established in 1924, Birdys was the first shop in Carrickmacross to sell newspapers when they first came into wide circulation. They were also one of the first to get a licence to sell tobacco in the days when a licence was needed. The shop came into Cathal's mother's family over 70 years ago, and has had several face-lifts since. The present facade was designed five years ago. They tried a modern look of aluminium but preferred to revert back to the old style traditional shop front. It proves to be an eye-catching attraction in Carrickmacross.

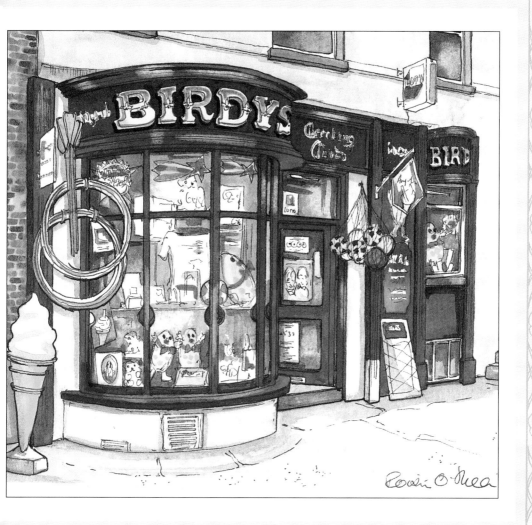

MAGEE'S SPIRIT STORE AND BAR, ENNISKILLEN, FERMANAGH

Brian Keane took over Magee's seven years ago from Mrs. Magee, who had been in charge for the previous fifty years. In times gone by, the back of the pub was a stagecoach yard – however, this was demolished to make way for a road. This pub would have been a staging post for messengers on horseback and also for coaches. Rooms and refreshment, including beer brewed and bottled on the premises would be available to passers-by. This pub would almost certainly have been a 'men only' establishment until relatively recently but now, with Mr. Keane in charge, it has become a very popular student pub. Although the focus of the pub has changed, the appearance has remained the same over the years.

POST OFFICE WINDOW

This painting is a detail of a replica post office in the Ulster American Folk Park in County Tyrone. The post office is part of a turn-of-the-century street scene faithfully recreated in this heritage centre which I would recommend visiting.

Issue of New Stamps

LICENSED & TO SELL
POSTAGE
AND INLAND REVENUE
STAMPS

V🜲R

O'DONOGHUE'S, DUBLIN

Famous for traditional music and fast service, O'Donoghue's pub is probably the most well-known drinking establishment in Ireland.

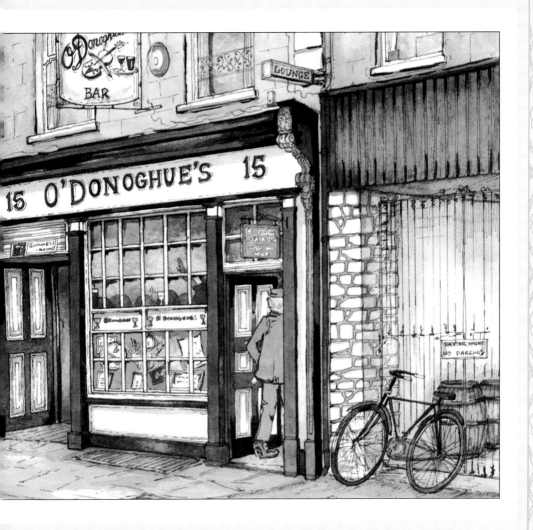

A. GUINNESS & SON

Somewhere in Ireland the gentle buzz of background conversation drifts through the murky depths of this old-style pub . . . I can't seem to remember just where it was!

OIFIG AN PHOIST

This old post office is 'just about' still in existence on Usher's Quay in Dublin, although I suspect it may manage to survive quite a few more years! The person peeping out the door is Mrs. Wall, who still runs this establishment and may or may not thank you for reminding her of this painting!

INDEX